HARDY LANDSCAPES

HARDY LANDSCAPES

Gordon Beningfield

VIKING

VIKING
Published by the Penguin Group
27 Wrights Lane, London W8 5TZ, England
Viking Penguin Inc., 40 West 23rd Street, New York, New York 10010, USA
Penguin Books Australia Ltd, Ringwood, Victoria, Australia
Penguin Books Canada Ltd, 2801 John Street, Markham, Ontario, Canada L3R 1B4
Penguin Books (NZ) Ltd, 182-190 Wairau Road, Auckland 10, New Zealand

Penguin Books Ltd, Registered Offices: Harmondsworth, Middlesex, England

First published 1990
10 9 8 7 6 5 4 3 2 1

Edited by Jill Hollis
Designed by Ian Cameron
Produced for Cameron Books,
2a Roman Way, London N7 8XG

Filmset in Linotype Baskerville by Cameron Books
Colour reproduction by La Cromolito, Milan
Monochrome reproduction by Gateway Platemakers, London
Printed and bound in Italy by Officine Grafiche Garzanti, Cernusco sul Naviglio

A CIP catalogue record for this book is available from the British Library.

ISBN 0-670-83211-1

Gordon Beningfield would like to acknowledge the help and encouragement given to him by
Gertrude Bugler, Diana Toms, Roger Peers, and Mr and Mrs T.W. Jesty.

Pictures

Preface

As a Dorset woman, born and bred, I, like countless others, including many native to the county, know and love the Dorset countryside. We are all deeply grateful to those who put it on permanent record; a gratitude felt most keenly by those, who, like myself, cannot now so easily get out and about in the countryside itself.

I am proud and privileged to have had the friendship of Thomas Hardy, who in prose and verse has left memorable pictures of Dorset which are and will be known throughout the world as long as our civilisation lasts.

I am grateful too, for the valued friendship of Gordon Beningfield, who, in books of illustrations of Dorset land and people has done with the brush something of what Hardy did with the pen. His delicate paintings are not only vivid and pictorially true, but they also breathe the spirit of Dorset. And now, in these pictures, so full of light and grace, we have the three together: Dorset, Hardy and Gordon Beningfield.

I can perhaps give this lovely book no higher praise than to say that I am quite sure that Hardy would not only have approved of it, but that it would have given to him, as it will to us all, deep and lasting pleasure.

Gertrude Bugler

Gertrude Bugler in the role of Tess in 1929

Thomas Hardy, aged eighty

In the early years of this century, the local amateur dramatic society in Dorchester put on various dramatisations of episodes from Thomas Hardy's works. Among the Hardy Players, as they came to be known, was a young actress called Gertrude Bugler, who became the star of the company and played several of Hardy's heroines, including Marty South in *The Woodlanders* in 1913 and Eustacia Vye in *The Return of the Native* in 1920. In 1924, Hardy's own stage adaptation of *Tess of the d'Urbervilles* was put on in Dorchester, and Mrs Bugler's performance as the tragic Tess Durbeyfield entranced not only him but some of the London critics who had made the journey especially to see the play. Plans were made to transfer the production to London, with the beautiful young actress in the title role. But a few months before the London rehearsals were due to start, Hardy's second wife, Florence Hardy, paid an unsolicited visit to Mrs Bugler and implored her to refuse the role, on the grounds that Hardy would insist on attending the London performances, and that this would endanger his health. Gertrude Bugler gracefully withdrew, allowing Hardy to believe that she had done so for the sake of her family. (She was, however, finally to play Tess in the West End with Mrs Hardy's blessing in 1929, a year after Thomas Hardy's death.) On hearing of her apparent change of heart, Hardy wrote to her saying, 'I do not believe that any London actress will represent Tess so nearly as I imagined her as you did.'

I have been privileged to spend many hours talking with Gertrude Bugler, and it is easy to see why Hardy was so captivated by her. Despite her ninety-three years, she is still extremely striking, with an indomitable spirit and a wonderful sense of humour. Quite recently I saw her after she had been extremely ill and was still very weak. As usual we talked about various places in Dorset that had associations with Hardy, and then suddenly she said, 'Well, it's no good just talking about the countryside, we'd better go and take another look.' And we set off on a trip through Hardy country that I shall never forget. Mrs Bugler clearly recollects the countryside as it was around Dorchester during her childhood and near Beaminster when she had moved there after her marriage. This contact with someone who knew Hardy, who interpreted the role of his most famous heroine to such effect during his lifetime and who has an intimate knowledge of the landscape which meant so much to him is a richer source of inspiration than anything I could have hoped for.

I started seriously pursuing my interest in Thomas Hardy twenty-five years ago. When I made my first trip to Dorset, I expected very little to be left of the scenery that was so vividly evoked by Hardy in his writings. But I discovered what was almost a dreamland of meadows, woodland, thickets, coppice, heathland, broad hedgerows flowing over into water-meadows, pools, streams and the remarkable range of wildlife that happily exists when all these habitats are left undisturbed. I have been going back at least three or four times a year ever since, so far never without a sense of excitement. People ask me why I don't live there, but I want it to remain a special place, far removed from everyday distractions. I go for one reason – to observe and work – and I want to be able to concentrate solely on that.

Even a hundred years ago, Hardy was aware of the threats faced by his beloved countryside, and urged people to value and preserve their natural inheritance. Too many interests are served by developing the countryside, instead of leaving it alone, for anybody to be complacent about the scale of possible destruction. Dorset may still retain more of the richness and variety of its landscape than has been saved elsewhere in southern England, but it is, like anywhere else, under siege. Local organisations and even individuals have made enormous efforts to safeguard their heritage, even buying up pieces of land that are of particular importance, and for this they deserve congratulation, but huge tracts of Dorset are so beautiful and irreplaceable that they deserve to be designated a national park. No better tribute could be paid to a writer who has delighted so many people with his evocations of the English countryside than affording proper protection to the heart of Hardy country. His readers and admirers should always be able to see for themselves that the dream-like landscapes he conjured up in his writings actually existed.

This book is a celebration of those landscapes, inspired not only by the more famous descriptions in the novels but also by Hardy's poetry, which, in his words, was 'the more individual part of my literary fruitage.'

Gordon Beningfield

In about 1800, Thomas Hardy's great-grandfather, John, built this house for his son. It was the first of what was to become a scattered hamlet of eight dwellings, and it was here, in Higher Bockhampton, known by some at that time as 'Cherry Alley' because of the cherry trees lining the lane through it, that Thomas Hardy was born, on 2nd June 1840. His earliest known poem describes the family home:

It faces west, and round the back and sides
High beeches, bending, hang a veil of boughs,
And sweep against the roof. Wild honeysucks
Climb on the walls, and seem to sprout a wish
(If we may fancy wish of trees and plants)
To overtop the apple-trees hard by.

Red roses, lilacs, variegated box
Are there in plenty, and such hardy flowers
As flourish best untrained. Adjoining these
Are herbs and esculents; and farther still
A field; then cottages with trees, and last
The distant hills and sky.

Behind, the scene is wilder. Heath and furze
Are everything that seems to grow and thrive
Upon the uneven ground. A stunted thorn
Stands here and there, indeed; and from a pit
An oak uprises, springing from a seed
Dropped by some bird a hundred years ago.

In days bygone –
Long gone – my father's mother, who is now
Blest with the blest, would take me out to walk.
At such a time I once inquired of her
How looked the spot when first she settled here.
The answer I remember. 'Fifty years
Have passed since then, my child, and change has marked
The face of all things. Yonder garden-plots
And orchards were uncultivated slopes
O'ergrown with bramble bushes, furze and thorn:
That road a narrow path shut in by ferns,
Which, almost trees, obscured the passer-by.

'Our house stood quite alone, and those tall firs
And beeches were not planted. Snakes and efts
Swarmed in the summer days, and nightly bats
Would fly about our bedrooms. Heathcroppers
Lived on the hills, and were our only friends;
So mild it was when first we settled here!'

Hardy records that the other houses in the hamlet 'were quaint, brass-knockered, and green-shuttered then, some with green garden-doors and white balls on the posts, and mainly occupied by lifeholders of substantial footing like the Hardys themselves . . . But the lifeholds fell into hand, and the quaint residences . . . have now perished every one, and have been replaced by labourers' brick cottages and other new farm buildings.'

Lifeholds were leases that usually lasted three generations and were non-renewable. They tended to be held by what Hardy describes in *Tess of the d'Urbervilles* as 'an interesting and better-informed class [than the agricultural labourers] . . . including the carpenter, the smith, the shoemaker, the huckster, together with nondescript workers, a set of people who owed a certain stability of aim and conduct to the fact of their being lifeholders . . .' In the case of Higher Bockhampton, the tenants were 'two retired military officers, one old navy lieutenant, a small farmer and tranter [part-time carrier], a relieving officer and registrar, and an old militiaman, whose wife was the monthly nurse that assisted Thomas Hardy into the world.'

Hardy saw that the stability resulting from a family having tenure for several generations meant that they 'formed the backbone of village life' and were 'the depositaries of the village traditions', which he counted as of great importance to the richness of life in the countryside. But he was also aware of the cruelty of a system which allowed a man to lose his birthplace without notice, usually, like Giles Winterborne, to see it razed to the ground by the landowner, for their 'independence of manner' meant that 'cottagers who were not directly employed on the land were looked upon with disfavour'.

Highly unusually, the Hardy family, whose lifehold should properly have determined on the death of Hardy's father, was allowed to renew the lease, and this accounts for the survival of the birthplace.

Hardy left Higher Bockhampton in 1862, but, finding that he missed his childhood home, returned in 1867 and lived there with his parents for much of the time until 1874, when he married Emma Gifford. Here he wrote five novels, including *Under the Greenwood Tree*, informing the editor of the magazine publishing *Far from the Madding Crowd* that 'I have decided to finish it here, which is within a walk of the district in which the incidents are supposed to occur. I find it a great advantage to be actually among the people described at the time of describing them.' Hardy wrote a large number of poems in which the house at Higher Bockhampton appears, many of which call up a certain nostalgia for the days when he lived there with his parents. I have chosen one depicting a scene that will be familiar to people who live in places quiet enough for birds to gather:

A Bird-Scene at a Rural Dwelling

When the inmate stirs, the birds retire discreetly
From the window-ledge, whereon they whistled sweetly
And on the step of the door,
In the misty morning hoar;
But now the dweller is up they flee
To the crooked neighbouring codlin-tree;
And when he comes fully forth they seek the garden,
And call from the lofty costard, as pleading pardon
For shouting so near before
In their joy at being alive:-
Meanwhile the hammering clock within goes five.

I know a domicile of brown and green,
Where for a hundred summers there have been
Just such enactments, just such daybreaks seen.

In *Under the Greenwood Tree*, Hardy models the tranter's home on his own and describes its appearance on Christmas Eve when the members of the Mellstock Quire are assembling there:

'It was a long low cottage with a hipped roof of thatch, having dormer windows breaking up into the eaves, a chimney standing in the middle of the ridge and another at each end. The window-shutters were not yet closed, and the fire- and candle-light within radiated forth upon the thick bushes of box and laurestinus growing in clumps outside, and upon the bare boughs of several codlin-trees hanging about in various distorted shapes, the result of early training as espaliers combined with careless climbing into their boughs in later years. The walls of the dwelling were for the most part covered with creepers, though these were rather beaten back from the doorway – a feature which was worn and scratched by much passing in and out, giving it by day the appearance of an old keyhole. Light streamed through the cracks and joints of outbuildings a little way from the cottage, a sight which nourished a fancy that the purpose of the erection must be rather to veil bright attractions than to shelter unsightly necessaries . . . at some little distance further a steady regular munching and the occasional scurr of a rope betokened a stable, and horses feeding within it.

'The choir stamped severally on the door-stone to shake from their boots any fragment of earth or leaf adhering thereto, then entered the house and looked around to survey the condition of things. Through the open doorway of a small inner room on the right hand, of a character between pantry and cellar, was Dick Dewy's father Reuben, by vocation a 'tranter', or irregular carrier . . . Being now occupied in bending over a hogshead that stood in the pantry ready horsed for the process of broaching, he did not take the trouble to turn or raise his eyes at the entry of his visitors, well knowing by their footsteps that they were the expected old comrades.

'The main room, on the left, was decked with bunches of holly and other evergreens, and from the middle of the beam bisecting the ceiling hung the mistletoe, of a size out of all proportion to the room, and extending so low that it became necessary for a full-grown person to walk round it in passing, or run the risk of entangling his hair. This apartment contained Mrs. Dewy the tranter's wife, and the four remaining children, Susan, Jim, Bessy, and Charles, graduating uniformly though at wide stages from the age of sixteen to that of four years . . .

'Mrs. Dewy sat in a brown settle by the side of the glowing wood fire – so glowing that with a heedful compression of the lips she would now and then rise and put her hand upon the hams and flitches of bacon lining the chimney, to reassure herself that they were not being broiled instead of smoked – a misfortune that had been known to happen now and then at Christmas-time . . . "Come in, come in, and draw up to the fire . . ." said Mrs. Dewy.'

Thomas Hardy's grandfather and father were both in the building business, but seem to have been at least as interested, if not more so, in providing the music at Stinsford Church as well as for any local event in need of musical entertainment. Christmas was, of course, the highpoint in the year:

'Conducting the church choir all the year round involved carol-playing and singing at Christmas . . . In addition to the ordinary practice, the work of preparing and copying carols a month of evenings beforehand was not light, and incidental expenses were appreciable. The parish being a large and scattered one, it was the custom of Thomas Hardy the First to assemble the rather perfunctory rank-and-file of the choir at his house; and this necessitated suppers, and suppers demanded (in those days) plenty of liquor. This was especially the case on Christmas Eve itself, when the rule was to go to the northern part of the parish and play at every house before supper; then to return to Bockhampton and sit over the meal till twelve o'clock, during which interval a good deal was consumed at the Hardys' expense, the choir being mainly poor men and hungry. They then started for the other parts of the parish, and did not get home till all was finished at about six in the morning, the performers themselves feeling "no more than malkins" [damp rags] in church next day, as they used to declare.'

The Hardys were, it seems, much in demand for their skilful string-playing, a tradition kept up by Thomas Hardy who was, it is said, greatly sought after for his uproarious fiddle-playing at local dances, an occupation recalled much later in the poem 'In the Small Hours':

> I lay in my bed and fiddled
> With a dreamland viol and bow,
> And the tunes flew back to my fingers
> I had melodied years ago.
> It was two or three in the morning
> When I fancy-fiddled so
> Long reels and country-dances,
> And hornpipes swift and slow.

In the painting are Hardy's violin (with the lion's head), together with his father's instrument and, on the right, his grandfather's bass-viol, all of which are now in the Dorset County Museum.

14

Ancient Cottages

Typical Dorset cottages. It was cottages like these, 'often as old as the parish church itself', that Hardy was anxious to see preserved. He estimated that they had been built in this style until the mid-nineteenth century, which was about the time when, as a child, he witnessed 'the building of what was probably one of the last of these old-fashioned cottages of "mudwall" and thatch. What was called mudwall was really a composition of chalk, clay, and straw – essentially, unbaked brick. This was mixed up into a sort of dough-pudding, close to where the cottage was to be built. The mixing was performed by treading and shovelling – women sometimes being called in to tread – and the straw was added to bind the mass together . . . It was then thrown up by pitchforks on to the wall, where it was trodden down, to a thickness of about two feet, till a "rise" of about three feet had been reached all round the building. This was left to settle for a day or two, and then another rise was effected, till the whole height to the wall plate was reached . . . When the wall had dried a little the outer face was cut down to a fairly flat surface with a spade, and the wall then plastered outside and in. The thatch projected sufficiently to prevent much rain running down the outer plaster, and even where it did run down the plaster was so hard as to be unaffected, more lime being used than nowadays.'

Many of these cottages were pulled down by landowners, who wished to replace them with more spacious, modern buildings of brick and slate and were astonished when the villagers expressed a preference for 'their dingy old hovels . . . with rooms only six feet high, and small dormer windows with little lead squares . . .' 'The explanation' wrote Hardy, 'is . . . that in the stroke of country winds a high room is not required for fresh air, sufficient ventilation entering through the door and window, and that the draught through the hollow brick wall makes the new cottages cold in winter.'

These extracts come from a pamphlet, published in 1927 by the Royal Society of Arts, called *The Preservation of Ancient Cottages*, to which Hardy and the then Prime Minister, Stanley Baldwin, contributed. Hardy ends by enjoining their owners to 'let as many as are left . . . remain where they are, and to repair them instead of replacing them with bricks, since, apart from their warmth and dryness, they have almost always great beauty and charm.'

Mellstock Church

The Hardy family had close connections with the church at Stinsford, or Mellstock, as it is called in its fictional appearances. At the very beginning of the nineteenth century, Hardy's grandfather took over the organisation of music at the church and, together with his two sons, played a leading role in the instrumental 'quire' there for some thirty-five years. Hardy remembered his mother's account of the sight of them on their way to Stinsford Church on Sunday mornings: 'They were always hurrying, being rather late, their fiddles and violoncello in green-baize bags under their left arms. They wore top hats, stick-up shirt-collars, dark blue coats with great collars and gilt buttons, deep cuffs and black silk "stocks" or neckerchiefs . . . My grandfather wore drab cloth breeches and buckled shoes, but his sons wore trousers and Wellington boots.'

'A Church Romance' expresses the first glimpses Hardy's mother had of his father:

> She turned in the high pew, until her sight
> Swept the west gallery, and caught its row
> Of music-men with viol, book, and bow
> Against the sinking sad tower-window light.
>
> She turned again; and in her pride's despite
> One strenuous viol's inspirer seemed to throw
> A message from his string to her below,
> Which said: 'I claim thee as my own forthright!'
>
> Thus their hearts' bond began, in due time signed.
> And long years thence, when Age had scared Romance,
> At some old attitude of his or glance
> That gallery-scene would break upon her mind,
> With him as minstrel, ardent, young, and trim,
> Bowing 'New Sabbath' or 'Mount Ephraim'.

Although the assembly of musicians at Stinsford was disbanded when Hardy was too young to know anything about it, he recreated a similar band in *Under the Greenwood Tree*, in the shape of the Mellstock Quire, no doubt wishing to celebrate what he saw as one more of the picturesque rural traditions which were fast disappearing. Certainly he was a devotee of traditional hymn tunes, and perhaps George Somerset in *A Laodicean* echoed Hardy's own feelings of attachment to these old melodies:

'He listened more heedfully. It was his old friend the "New Sabbath", which he had never once heard since the lisping days of his childhood, and whose existence, much as it had then been to him, he had till this moment quite forgotten. Where the "New Sabbath" had kept itself all those years – why that sound and hearty melody had disappeared from all the cathedrals, parish churches, minster and chapels-of-ease that he had been acquainted with during his apprenticeship of life . . . he could not at first, say. But then he recollected that the tune appertained to the old west-gallery period of church-music . . . that old time when the repetition of a word, or half-line of a verse, was not considered a disgrace to an ecclesiastical choir.'

'Afternoon Service at Mellstock', which again puts in a word for the old psalmody, also conjures up an idyllic view of rural church-going:

> On afternoons of drowsy calm
> We stood in the panelled pew,
> Singing one-voiced a Tate-and-Brady psalm
> To the tune of 'Cambridge New'.
>
> We watched the elms, we watched the rooks,
> The clouds upon the breeze,
> Between the whiles of glancing at our books,
> And swaying like the trees . . .

Hardy's attachment to traditional church-going is clear, and like the rest of his family he did much to support it, singing in Stinsford choir after the instrumental band had disappeared. But he was in the end an agnostic, and a clue to one of the reasons for his disillusionment is perhaps contained in a rather satirical poem entitled 'In Church':

> 'And now to God the Father,' he ends,
> And his voice thrills up to the topmost tiles:
> Each listener chokes as he bows and bends,
> And emotion pervades the crowded aisles.
> Then the preacher glides to the vestry-door,
> And shuts it, and thinks he is seen no more.
>
> The door swings softly ajar meanwhile,
> And a pupil of his in the Bible class,
> Who adores him as one without gloss or guile,
> Sees her idol stand with a satisfied smile
> And re-enact at the vestry glass
> Each pulpit gesture in deft dumb-show
> That had moved the congregation so.

For Hardy, Stinsford Church, or more particularly, its churchyard, had a significance that reached back beyond the time of the 'church-players' and continued to grow long after their demise. His grandfather was buried close to *his* father and mother, 'and near the knights of various dates in the sixteenth and eighteenth centuries, with whom the Hardys had been connected', and, over time, not only Hardy's parents but also his sister Mary and first wife Emma Lavinia were laid to rest there, just across the mead from Max Gate, the house Hardy built for himself. Nine years after Hardy's death, Florence, his second wife, was to be buried there too. Emma's grave, in particular, became the focus for numerous poems for, in spite of the coolness which seems to have existed between them for much of their marriage, her death provoked a seemingly unquenchable flow of nostalgia, wistfulness and regret in Hardy:

> Woman much missed, how you call to me, call to me,
> Saying that now you are not as you were
> When you had changed from the one who was all to me,
> But as at first, when our day was fair.
>
> Can it be you that I hear? Let me view you, then,
> Standing as when I drew near to the town.
> Where you would wait for me: yes, as I knew you then,
> Even to the original air-blue gown!
>
> Or is it only the breeze in its listlessness
> Travelling across the wet mead to me here,
> You being ever dissolved to wan listlessness,
> Heard no more again far or near?
>
> Thus I; faltering forward,
> Leaves around me falling,
> Wind oozing thin through the thorn from norward,
> And the woman calling.

In another poem, he imagines his dead wife's upbraiding:

> Now I am dead you come to me
> In the moonlight, comfortless,
> Ah, what would I have given alive
> To win such tenderness!

But in still another he comforts himself:

> . . . I hear the notes as when
> Once she sang to me:
> 'O the dream that thou art my Love, be it thine,
> And the dream that I am thy Love, be it mine,
> And death may come, but Loving is divine.'

With a lighter touch, Hardy remembers other women, who were also buried in the churchyard and who had moved him in his youth:

> I am forgetting Louie the buoyant;
> Why not raise her phantom, too,
> Here in daylight
> With the elect one's
> She will never thrust the foremost figure out of view!

Louie was 'Louisa in the Lane', a farmer's daughter whom he had longed for but been too bashful to approach. In a poem composed a few months before his death, he wrote,

> Meet me again as at that time
> In the hollow of the lane;
> I will not pass as in my prime
> I passed at each day's wane. . .

Another late poem, 'Voices from Things Growing in a Churchyard', refers to an old school companion of Hardy, Fanny Hurden, who was of fragile health and died at the age of eighteen:

> These flowers are I, poor Fanny Hurd,
> Sir or Madam,
> A little girl here sepultured.
> Once I flit-fluttered like a bird
> Above the grass, as now I wave
> In daisy shapes above my grave,
> All day cheerily,
> All night eerily!

Weatherbury

Weatherbury, or Puddletown, as the real village is called, is the setting for much of the action in *Far from the Madding Crowd*. Hardy knew it well. Many of his relatives lived there, including an aunt whose 'amazement was great' when he and his mother arrived to see her one afternoon in disguise having walked across the heath with cabbage-nets wrapped over their faces, and Tryphena Sparks, a cousin sometimes thought to have been an erstwhile love of Hardy because of his description of her (in a poem written on hearing of her death) as 'my lost prize . . . whom I knew when her dreams were upbrimming with light'.

In Hardy's youth, Puddletown was a small but important commercial centre providing most of the basic services and shops needed by a rural community. When he wrote *Far from the Madding Crowd*, he was aware that life was already beginning to change there, and he was anxious to record what he saw as the untouched nature of life in this part of Dorset:

'In comparison with cities, Weatherbury was immutable. The Citizen's *Then* is the rustic's *Now*. In London, twenty or thirty years ago are old times; in Paris ten years, or five; in Weatherbury three or four score years were included in the mere present, and nothing less than a century set a mark on its face or tone. Five decades hardly modified the cut of a gaiter, the embroidery of a smock-frock, by the breadth of a hair. Ten generations failed to alter the turn of a single phrase. In these Wessex nooks the busy outsider's ancient times are only old; his old times are still new; his present is futurity.'

By the end of the century, the scenes against which the story had been set were 'hardly discernible'. In his preface to the novel, Hardy commented on the transformations wrought in the place:

'The practice of divination by Bible and key [a superstition indulged in by Bathsheba], the regarding of Valentines as things of serious import, the shearing-supper, the long smock-frocks, and the harvest home, have, too, nearly disappeared in the wake of the old houses; and with them has gone, it is said, much of that love of fuddling to which the village at one time was notoriously prone. The change at the root of this has been the recent supplanting of the class of stationary cottagers, who carried on the local traditions and humours, by a population of more or less migratory labourers, which has led to a break of continuity in local history, more fatal than any other thing to the preservation of legend, folk-lore, close inter-social relations, and eccentric individualities. For those the indispensable conditions of existence are attachment to the soil of one particular spot by generation after generation.'

After Troy discovered that Fanny Robin had died while giving birth to his child in Casterbridge workhouse, and was to be buried at Weatherbury, he used 'all the money he possessed' to buy a marble headstone for her. At ten o'clock the same evening he took a basket laden with flower roots to the churchyard:

'Troy laid these out upon the grass, and with an impassive face set to work to plant them. The snowdrops were arranged in a line on the outside of the coping, the remainder within the enclosure of the grave. The crocuses and hyacinths were to grow in rows: some of the summer flowers he placed over her head and feet, the lilies and forget-me-nots over her heart . . .'

Just before midnight, rain began to fall. Feeling weary and seeing that the weather was worsening, Troy decided to retreat to the north porch of the church for the night, resolving to finish his work in the morning. During the night the rain fell steadily, and a rain-water pipe on top of the church tower produced a 'persistent torrent from the gargoyle's jaws [that] directed all its vengeance into the grave.'

In the morning, 'Fanny's repentant lover' awoke to bright sunshine and made his way to the grave. 'At one place in the path he saw a tuft of stringy roots washed white and clean as a bundle of tendons. He picked it up – surely it could not be one of the primroses he had planted? He saw a bulb, another, and another as he advanced. Beyond doubt they were the crocuses. With a face of perplexed dismay Troy turned the corner and then beheld the wreck the stream had made.' He was completely unnerved: 'The planting of flowers on Fanny's grave had been perhaps but a species of elusion of the primary grief, and now it was as if his intention had been known and circumvented . . . He did not attempt to fill up the hole, replace the flowers or do anything at all. He simply threw up his cards and forswore his game for that time and always.'

At the end of the novel, after the murder of Troy by Farmer Boldwood, Weatherbury Church is the scene of the marriage of Bathsheba and Gabriel Oak, desired by Bathsheba to be 'the most private, secret, plainest wedding that it is possible to have.' The couple, Oak wearing a great coat and Bathsheba in a cloak that reached her clogs, walk to church under their umbrellas 'arm in arm for the first time in their lives.'

22

In *Under the Greenwood Tree*, Hardy describes the kind of instrumental choir or band that his father, and grandfather, who played the violin and the bass viol, took part in. The gallery in Stinsford Church (on which Mellstock church was based) has long since been removed, but the church at Puddletown, which Hardy also knew well and called Weatherbury, still has one, no doubt very similar to the structure that the Mellstock Quire inhabited.

'The gallery of Mellstock Church had a status and sentiment of its own. A stranger there was regarded with a feeling altogether differing from that of the congregation below towards him. Banished from the nave as an intruder whom no originality could make interesting, he was received above as a curiosity that no unfitness could render dull. The gallery, too, looked down upon and knew the habits of the nave to its remotest peculiarity, and had an extensive stock of exclusive information about it; whilst the nave knew nothing of the gallery folk, as gallery folk, beyond their loud-sounding minims and chest notes. Such topics as that the clerk was always chewing tobacco except at the moment of crying amen; that he had a dust-hole in his pew; that during the sermon certain young daughters of the village had left off caring to read anything so mild as the marriage service for some years, and now regularly studied the one which chronologically follows it; that a pair of lovers touched fingers through a knot-hole between their pews in the manner ordained by their great exemplars,

Pyramus and Thisbe; that Mrs. Ledlow, the farmer's wife, counted her money and reckoned her week's marketing expenses during the first lesson – all news to those below – were stale subjects here.

'Old William sat in the centre of the front row, his violoncello between his knees and two singers on each hand. Behind him on the left, came the treble singers and Dick; and on the right the tranter and the tenors. Further back was old Mail with the altos and supernumeraries.'

The Mellstock Quire would have been unamused by any comparison with their Weatherbury counterparts whose use of 'serpents' and 'clar'nets' (instead of a purely string band) they despised:

' "Robert Penny, you was in the right," broke in the eldest Dewy. "They should ha' stuck to strings. Your brass-man is a rafting dog – well and good; your reed-man is a dab at stirring ye – well and good; your drum-man is a rare bowel-shaker – good again. But I don't care who hears me say it, nothing will spak to your heart wi' the sweetness o' the man of strings!"
"Strings for ever!" said little Jimmy.'

The group of instruments below (all in the Dorset County Museum) might well have been played by the Weatherbury instrumentalists – two clarinets, a trumpet, a double flageolet and a hum-strum, a homemade instrument that made a droning noise and was played with a horse-hair bow.

Sturminster Newton

In the summer of 1876, two years after they married and six years after they first met, Thomas and Emma Hardy moved into the first house they had had to themselves, 'a pretty cottage overlooking the Dorset Stour – called "Riverside Villa" . . . at Sturminster Newton.' They quickly furnished it, 'in part by going to Bristol and buying £100 worth of mid-Victorian furniture in two hours'. The Hardys spent almost two years here while Hardy wrote *The Return of the Native* and enjoyed what appears to have been a charmed existence. Much later Hardy was to look back on this time, with great nostalgia and regret at its passing, in 'A Two-Years' Idyll':

> Yes; such it was;
> Just those two seasons unsought,
> Sweeping like summertide wind on our ways;
> Moving, as straws,
> Hearts quick as ours in those days;
> Going like wind, too, and rated as nought
> Save as the prelude to plays
> Soon to come – larger, life-fraught:
> Yes; such it was.
>
> 'Nought' it was called,
> Even by ourselves – that which springs
> Out of the years for all flesh, first or last,
> Commonplace, scrawled
> Dully on days that go past.
> Yet, all the while, it up bore us like wings
> Even in hours overcast:
> Aye, though this best thing of things,
> 'Nought' it was called!
>
> What seems it now?
> Lost: such beginning was all;
> Nothing came after: romance straight forsook
> Quickly somehow
> Life when we sped from our nook,
> Primed for new scenes with designs smart and tall . . .
> – A preface without any book,
> A trumpet uplipped, but no call;
> That seems it now.

Notes made by Hardy shortly after the young couple's arrival at their new home testify to his delight in the place: 'Rowed on the Stour in the evening, the sun setting up the river. Just afterwards a faint exhalation visible on surface of water as we stirred it with the oars. A fishy smell from the numerous eels and other fish beneath. Mowers salute us. Rowed among the water-lilies to gather them. Their long ropy stems. . .

'Passing the island drove out a flock of swallows from the bushes and sedge, which had gone there to roost. Gathered meadow-sweet. Rowed with difficulty through the weeds, the rushes on the border standing like palisades against the bright sky . . . A cloud in the sky like a huge quill-pen.'

In March 1878, as they were leaving for London in the interests of furthering Hardy's career as a novelist, he recorded: 'End of the Sturminster Newton Idyll . . .' to which he later added 'Our happiest time'.

The scene I have painted remains almost as tranquil as it must have been on the day described by Hardy in 'The Musical Box' when he 'walked by Stourside Mill, where broad stream-lilies throng.'

Forty years after he first moved to Sturminster Newton, Hardy returned, and it was probably this visit, made with his second wife, that prompted him to write several poems evoking lost pleasures there, including 'The Second Visit', which expresses the disappointment of going back to a familiar place with which one no longer has any real links:

> Clack, clack, clack, went the mill-wheel as I came,
> And she was on the bridge with the thin handrail,
> And the miller at the door, and the ducks at mill-tail;
> I come again years after, and all there seems the same.
>
> And so indeed it is: the apple-tree'd old house,
> And the deep mill-pond, and the wet wheel clacking,
> And a woman on the bridge, and white ducks quacking,
> And the miller at the door, powdered pale from boots to brows.
>
> But it's not the same miller whom long ago I knew,
> Nor are they the same apples, nor the same drops that dash
> Over the wet wheel, nor the ducks below that splash,
> Nor the woman who to fond plaints replied, 'You know I do!'

Hardy was brought up in a cottage right on the edge of a large expanse of heathland. His mother remembered a curious detail of his early life. One hot afternoon, she found her infant son asleep in his cradle with 'a large snake curled up upon his breast, comfortably asleep like himself. It had crept into the house from the heath hard by . . .' Clym Yeobright's relationship with the heath in *The Return of the Native* may well reflect some of Hardy's feelings: 'His eyes had first opened thereon; with its appearance all the first images of his memory were mingled; his estimate of life had been coloured by it . . .' Certainly this kind of countryside held an attraction for him unlike that of any other: 'It was a spot,' he remarks, 'which returned upon the memory of those who loved it with an aspect of peculiar and kindly congruity.'

Here, perhaps more than in any other part of the Wessex landscape, he was aware of the ancient history of this 'obscure, obsolete, superseded country':

'To recline on a stump of thorn in the central valley of Egdon between afternoon and night, as now, where the eye could reach nothing of the world outside the summits and shoulders of heathland which filled the whole circumference of its glance, and to know that everything around and underneath had been from prehistoric times as unaltered as the stars overhead, gave ballast to the mind adrift on change, and harassed by the irrepressible New . . . The sea changed, the fields changed, the rivers, the villages, and the people changed, yet Egdon remained.'

In *The Mayor of Casterbridge*, when Elizabeth-Jane and Donald Farfrae go off in search of Henchard, they are directed along a road on the north side of Egdon Heath and are soon 'bowling across that ancient country whose surface never had stirred to a finger's depth, save by the scratching of rabbits, since brushed by the feet of the earliest tribes.'

The wild, unspoilt nature of the place had a great deal to do with the absence of human intervention – a fact of which Hardy was only too well aware: 'Not a plough had ever disturbed a grain of that stubborn soil. In the heath's barrenness to the farmer lay its fertility to the historian. There had been no obliteration, because there had been no tending.' But this description of 'the vast tract of unenclosed wild known as Egdon Heath' from *The Return of the Native* is evoking a landscape that had already started to vanish in Hardy's day, largely as a result of the Acts of Enclosure. 'Under the general name of "Egdon Heath",' explained Hardy, '. . . are united or typified heaths of various real names, to the number of at least a dozen; these being virtually one in character and aspect, though their original unity, or partial unity, is now somewhat disguised by intrusive strips and

slices brought under the plough . . . or planted to woodland.' One cannot help thinking that Hardy shared with Clym Yeobright 'a barbarous satisfaction at observing that, in some of the attempts at reclamation from the waste, tillage, after holding on for a year or two, had receded again in despair, the ferns and furze-tufts stubbornly reasserting themselves.'

Now, the process so regretted by Hardy has taken hold to such an extent that there are only two small, isolated chunks of heathland left: one near Corfe Castle and the other near Wareham, and conifers have been planted right up to the back of the birthplace. As a result of bitter complaint, not least concerning the risk of fire, the Forestry Commission has cleared a small area immediately behind the cottage, but when people come from all over the world to see the wild heathland that extended for miles from Hardy's back door, all they can see is Christmas trees.

In *The Return of the Native*, after Clym Yeobright had, with great sadness, left his mother's home because of her strong disapproval of his love for Eustacia Vye, he set out to meet the recipient of his affections:

'It was a sunny afternoon at the beginning of summer and the moist hollows of the heath had passed from their brown to their green stage . . . In the minor valleys, between the hillocks which diversified the contour of the vale, the fresh young ferns were luxuriantly growing up ultimately to reach a height of five or six feet. He descended a litle way, flung himself down in a spot where a path emerged from one of the small hollows, and waited . . . He was in a nest of vivid green. The ferny vegetation round him, though so abundant, was quite uniform . . . The air was warm with a vaporous warmth and the stillness was unbroken. Lizards, grasshoppers and ants were the only living things to be beheld.'

The two met, decided they should marry without further ado, and then went their separate ways as dusk fell, with Clym somewhat overwhelmed by events but 'fully alive to the beauty of that untarnished early summer green which was worn for the nonce by the poorest blade.'

For a tragically short time, Clym and Eustacia were rapturously happy – 'They were like those double stars which revolve round each other, and from a distance appear to be one' – and it is the evocation of the heath at this time that I wanted to reflect in this painting: 'The July sun shone over Egdon and fired its crimson heather to scarlet. It was the one season of the year, and the one weather of the season, in which the heath was joyous.'

'Only in summery days of lightest feather did its mood touch the level of gaiety', remarks Hardy, and certainly for much of the novel it is the more sombre aspect of the heath that is evoked:

'Twilight combined with the scenery of Egdon Heath to evolve a thing majestic without severity, impressive without showiness, emphatic in its admonitions, grand in its simplicity . . . Fair prospects wed happily with fair times; but alas, if times be not fair! Men have oftener suffered from the mockery of a place too smiling for their reason than from the oppression of surroundings oversadly tinged. Haggard Egdon appealed to a subtler and scarcer instinct, to a more recently learnt emotion, than that which responds to the sort of beauty called charming and fair.'

For some of the characters, not least those for whom times were far from fair, Egdon had a threatening and oppressive side, 'a place which had slipped out of its century generations ago, to intrude as an uncouth object into this.' When, in *The Hand of Ethelberta*, Mountclere and his companions had driven across 'these eternal heaths under the eternally drumming storm' for ten to twelve miles, they were still confronted by 'the everlasting heath, the black hills bulging against the sky, the barrows upon their round summits like warts on a swarthy skin'. In *The Withered Arm*, when Rhoda Brook led Gertrude Lodge 'into the interior of this solemn country' to consult Conjuror Trendle on how to restore Mrs Lodge's mysteriously wasted arm, 'thick clouds made the atmosphere dark, though it was as yet only early afternoon; and the wind howled dismally over the slopes of the heather – not improbably the same heath which had witnessed the agony of the Wessex King Ina, presented to after ages as Lear.' Rushy Pond, where Gertrude Lodge paused on her way to Casterbridge, and saw – in the distance – the preparations being made for the hanging that was to take place there the next day, can still be seen just a third of a mile from Hardy's birthplace.

' "I like what I was born near to;" ' says Thomasin, in *The Return of the Native*, when her husband asks 'with pitying surprise' whether she likes the heath, ' "I admire its grim old face" ', a sentiment almost certainly shared by Hardy, for whom it had something close to spiritual significance:

'It was a place perfectly accordant with man's nature – neither ghastly, hateful, nor ugly: neither commonplace, unmeaning, nor tame; but like man, slighted and enduring, and withal singularly colossal and mysterious in its swarthy monotony. As with some persons who have long lived apart, solitude seemed to look out of its countenance. It had a lonely face, suggesting tragical possibilities . . .'

Today, the surviving fragments of heath are still, as Thomasin put it, 'a nice wild place to walk in'. One evening, after spending a day walking with a friend near Wareham, I realised how close we were to the heath, and, on impulse, went on to it. Dusk was falling and suddenly we heard a curious chirring noise. Within a very short time, we saw, perched on top of some gorse nearby, a night-jar or, as Hardy would have said, a dewfall-hawk. This was a gift of an image, because it matched one of the descriptions in 'Afterwards' so exactly:

When the Present has latched its postern behind my tremulous stay,
And the May month flaps its glad green leaves like wings,
Delicate-filmed as new-spun silk, will the neighbours say,
'He was a man who used to notice such things'?

If it be in the dusk when, like an eyelid's soundless blink,
The dewfall-hawk comes crossing the shades to alight
Upon the wind-warped upland thorn, a gazer may think,
'To him this must have been a familiar sight.'

If I pass during some nocturnal blackness, mothy and warm,
When the hedgehog travels furtively over the lawn,
One may say, 'he strove that such innocent creatures should come
    to no harm,
But he could do little for them; and now he is gone.'

If, when hearing that I have been stilled at last, they stand at the door,
Watching the full-starred heavens that winter sees,
Will this thought rise on those who will meet my face no more,
'He was one who had an eye for such mysteries'?

And will any say when my bell of quittance is heard in the gloom,
And a crossing breeze cuts a pause in its outrollings,
Till they rise again, as they were a new bell's boom,
'He hears it not now, but used to notice such things'?

The Fruitful Ground

'And so the infatuated surgeon went along through the gorgeous autumn landscape of White-Hart Vale, surrounded by orchards lustrous with the reds of apple-crops, berries, and foliage, the whole intensified by the gilding of the declining sun. The earth this year had been prodigally bountiful, and now was the supreme moment of her bounty. In the poorest spots the hedges were bowed with haws and blackberries; acorns cracked underfoot, and the burst husks of chestnuts lay exposing their auburn contents as if arranged by anxious sellers in a fruit-market.'

This glorious description comes from *The Woodlanders* and is what inspired me to paint this picture. The 'infatuated surgeon' was Edred Fitzpiers, who had won and married the gentle Grace Melbury, but then became fixed on another woman – to whom he was riding at this moment. The beauty of the landscape stands in keen contrast to the mess of human relations within it.

The 'fruity district of deep loam' is where much of *The Woodlanders* is set; this is cider apple country, 'where the people make the best cider and cider wine in all Wessex', evoked with great lyricism by Hardy, often through the character of Giles Winterborne, the man who had always loved Grace:

'He looked and smelt like Autumn's very brother, his face being sunburnt to wheat-colour, his eyes blue as corn-flowers, his sleeves and leggings dyed with fruit-stains, his hands clammy with the sweet juice of apples, his hat sprinkled with pips, and everywhere about him that atmosphere of cider which at its first return each season has such an indescribable fascination for those who have been born and bred among the orchards.'

This was a fascination certainly shared by Hardy, who had helped at his father's cider-making, 'a proceeding he had always enjoyed from childhood' and 'a work whose sweet smells and oozings in the crisp autumn air can never be forgotten by those who have a hand in it.' Details that show his knowledge of this rural occupation crop up in other stories. For his son's wedding in *The Trumpet Major*, Mr Loveday laid in a hogshead of fine cider 'pressed from fruit judiciously chosen by an old hand – Horner and Cleeves apple for the body, a few Tom-Putts for colour, and just a dash of Old Five-corners for sparkle', and, in *Under the Greenwood Tree*, 'a drop of the right sort' is made from 'Sansoms, Stubbards, five-corners . . . [and] a sprinkling of they that grow down by the orchard rails'.

Giles Winterborne was an itinerant cider-maker, travelling with his press and mill fixed on wheels to places like Sherton Abbey 'on the margin of Pomona's plain', where there was no cider-making apparatus, 'and with a couple of horses, buckets, tubs, strainers and an assistant or two, he wandered from place to place, deriving very satisfactory returns for his trouble in such a prolific season as the present.'

Grace, newly married to Fitzpiers, watched Winterborne's applemill and press being erected in the yard of the hotel where she was staying.

'. . . beyond the yard were to be seen gardens and orchards now bossed, nay encrusted, with scarlet and gold fruit, stretching to infinite distance under a luminous lavender mist. The time was early autumn,

> "When the fair apples, red as evening sky,
> Do bend the tree unto the fruitful ground,
> When juicy pears, and berries of black dye
> Do dance in air, and call the eyes around." '

Max Gate

This is Max Gate, the Victorian villa designed by Hardy and built for him by his father and brother by 1885. The name of the house came from that of an old keeper of a tollgate nearby called Mack. It is characteristic of Hardy to have wanted to give his new home a link with the past. A visitor to the house the year after it was completed remarked that 'from its position [it is] almost the first object in the neighbourhood to catch the sun's morning rays, and the last to relinquish the evening glow . . .'

When the Hardys moved in, the house, built on upland 'as lonely as it is elevated', must have felt somewhat exposed:

'The house is bleak and cold
Built so new for me!
All the winds upon the wold
Search it through for me;
No screening trees abound,
And the curious eyes around,
Keep on view for me.'

Always needful of privacy, as well as quiet, Hardy planted between two and three thousand trees around the house, which are no doubt those referred to in 'At Day-Close in November':

> The ten hours' light is abating,
> And a late bird wings across,
> Where the pines, like waltzers waiting,
> Give their black heads a toss.
>
> Beech leaves, that yellow the noon-time,
> Float past like specks in the eye;
> I set every tree in my June time,
> And now they obscure the sky . . .

It is easy to imagine Hardy looking out of the window of his study – the upstairs room in the sketch on the right – and musing on how the trees have grown over the years.

At the age of eighty-two, Hardy wrote a poem which reveals how he missed his first wife, Emma, with whom he had shared Max Gate for twenty-seven years until her death in 1912.

> 'Tis ten years since
> I saw her on the stairs
> Heard her in house-affairs,
> And listened to her cares;
> And the trees are ten feet taller,
> And the sunny spaces smaller
> Whose bloomage would enthrall her;
> And the piano wires are rustier,
> The smell of bindings mustier,
> And lofts and lumber dustier
> Than when, with casual look
> And ear, light note I took
> Of what shut like a book
> Those ten years since!

The study of the garden door is a painting I call 'The Secret Escape'. This door led out of the garden into the lane and the countryside beyond. When visitors arrived unexpectedly, which they increasingly did as his fame grew, and Hardy felt that he could not bear the disturbance of dealing with yet another caller, he would tell the maid he was slipping out of the house so that she could say that Mr Hardy wasn't in. Then he could creep out, probably through the vegetable patch and past the fruit trees, perhaps taking his dog Wessex with him.

When Tess had returned to her parents' home after her ill treatment at the hands of Alec d'Urberville, she first attempted to continue her life as normal, but was soon humiliated by the whispering in the village about what had happened to her. She retreated from view, scarcely stirring from the cottage: 'So close kept she that at length almost everybody thought she had gone away.'

Many months later, after the birth of her illegitimate child, Tess joined the other women from the village in the fields to help with the harvest. Hardy characteristically supplies an accurate description of the operations involved. Because the reaper could not work right to the edges of the field, a lane of a few feet wide had to be hand-cut all the way round, after which work began in earnest: the machine reaped the corn and left behind it small heaps, which had to be gathered by hand into sheaves. This was a job done mainly by young women who 'wore drawn cotton bonnets with great flapping curtains to keep off the sun and gloves to prevent their hands being wounded by the stubble.'

Tess worked hard:

'Her binding proceeds with clock-like monotony. From the sheaf last finished she draws a handful of ears, patting their tips with her left palm to bring them even. Then stooping low she moves forward, gathering the corn with both hands against her knees, and pushing her left gloved hand under the bundle to meet the right on the other side, holding the corn in an embrace like that of a lover. She brings the ends of the bond together, and kneels on the sheaf while she ties it, beating back her skirts now and then when lifted by the breeze. A bit of her naked arm is visible between the buff leather of the gauntlet and the sleeve of her gown; and as the day wears on its feminine smoothness becomes scarified by the stubble, and bleeds.'

'At intervals she stands up to rest, and to retie her disarranged apron, or to pull her bonnet straight. Then one can see the oval face of a handsome young woman with deep dark eyes and long heavy clinging tresses, which seem to clasp in a beseeching way anything they fall against. . .'

'The movements of the other women were more or less similar to Tess's, the whole bevy of them drawing together like dancers in a quadrille at the completion of a sheaf by each, every one placing her sheaf on end against those of the rest, till a shock, or "stitch" as it was here called, of ten or a dozen was formed.'

Just before eleven o'clock, a group of children arrived carrying 'what at first sight seemed to be a doll, but proved to be an infant in long clothes and some lunch . . . The harvesters ceased working, took their provisions, and sat down against one of the shocks. Here they fell to, the men plying a stone jar freely, and passing round a cup.' Tess took the baby and 'with a curiously stealthy yet courageous movement, and with a still rising colour, unfastened her frock and began suckling the child.'

In *The Mayor of Casterbridge*, there is a late and troublesome harvest.

'The fact was, that no sooner had the sickles begun to play than the atmosphere suddenly felt as if cress would grow in it without other nourishment. It rubbed people's cheeks like damp flannel when they walked abroad. There was a gusty, high, warm wind . . .'

The capricious weather had delayed the harvest so seriously that when a fine day dawned, as many people as possible went out to salvage what they could of the crops:

'Nearly the whole town had gone into the fields. The Casterbridge populace still retained the primitive habit of helping one another in time of need; and thus, though the corn belonged to the farming section of the little community – that inhabiting the Durnover quarter – the remainder was no less interested in the labour of getting it home.'

After Tess's baby suddenly died, 'a waif to whom eternal Time had been a matter of days merely', her life drifted on, but over time she felt that to escape the past, she had to move away from the village where she had been brought up: 'A particularly fine spring came round, and the stir of germination was almost audible in the buds; it moved her, as it moved the wild animals, and made her passionate to go.'

On hearing that a dairy-house 'many miles southward' required a milk-maid, she decided to leave the Blackmoor Vale and offer herself for the job. 'On one point she was resolved: there should be no more d'Urberville air-castles in the dreams and deeds of her new life. She would be the dairy-maid Tess, and nothing more.'

This is a scene from the Valley of the Great Dairies where Tess spent some of the happiest days of her life, working from spring to autumn as a dairymaid for Dairyman Crick and being courted by Angel Clare. The cattle that graze there nowadays are more likely to be Friesians than the brown and white beasts tended by Tess, but it is still possible to call up some of the atmosphere that she experienced so keenly as she first surveyed her new home:

'It was intrinsically different from the Vale of Little Dairies, Blackmoor Vale, which . . . she had exclusively known till now. The world was drawn to a larger pattern here. The enclosures numbered fifty acres instead of ten, the farmsteads were more extended, the groups of cattle formed tribes hereabout; there only families. These myriads of cows stretching under her eyes from the far east to the far west outnumbered any she had ever seen at one glance before . . . The ripe hue of the red and dun kine absorbed the evening sunlight, which the white-coated animals returned to the eye in rays almost dazzling, even at the distant elevation on which she stood.

'The bird's-eye perspective before her was not so luxuriantly beautiful, perhaps, as that other one which she knew so well; yet it was more cheering. It lacked the intensely blue atmosphere of the rival vale, and its heavy soils and scents; the new air was clear, bracing, ethereal. The river itself, which nourished the grass and cows of these renowned dairies, flowed not like the streams in Blackmoor. Those were slow, silent, often turbid; flowing over beds of mud into which the incautious wader might sink and vanish unawares. The Froom waters were clear as the pure River of Life shown to the Evangelist, rapid as the shadow of a cloud, with pebbly shallows that prattled to the sky all day long. There the water-flower was the lily; the crowfoot here.'

I had wanted to paint one of the little footbridges that Angel and Tess wandered over as they courted in the meads, but had lost hope of finding one until I suddenly came across this bridge, clearly maintained, in the traditional manner, by using materials found to hand in the countryside.

'. . . during this October month of wonderful afternoons they roved along the meads by creeping paths which followed the brinks of trickling tributary brooks, hopping across by little wooden bridges to the other side, and back again. They were never out of the sound of some purling weir, whose buzz accompanied their own murmuring, while the beams of the sun, almost as horizontal as the mead itself, formed a pollen of radiance over the landscape. They saw tiny blue fogs in the shadows of trees and hedges, all the time that there was bright sunshine elsewhere. The sun was so near the ground, and the sward so flat, that the shadows of Clare and Tess would stretch a quarter of a mile ahead of them, like two long fingers pointing afar to where the green alluvial reaches abutted against the sloping sides of the vale.'

Dairying

Two images related to Tess's time as a dairymaid, which I find a compelling subject. The cattle she tended would have been either Red Devons or Dairy Shorthorns, as referred to in 'The Milkmaid':

> Under a daisied bank
> There stands a rich red ruminating cow,
> And hard against her flank
> A cotton-hooded milkmaid bends her brow.
>
> The flowery river-ooze
> Upheaves and falls; milk purrs in the pail;
> Few pilgrims but would choose
> The peace of such a life in such a vale.
>
> The maid breathes words – to vent,
> It seems, her sense of Nature's scenery,
> Of whose life, sentiment,
> And essence, very part itself is she . . .

I have painted a Shorthorn partly because of Ron, a Dorset farmer I know. Down in Powerstock, he farms in a way that Hardy might well have approved of. Every day, except in winter, he takes his cattle, many of which are Shorthorns, through the village and down to the apple orchards to graze. He is a man with a huge knowledge of farming techniques that some people might see as old-fashioned, but which I think are the true skills of the countryside. Vast areas of Hardy's heartland have changed, but small pockets survive, and in a way Ron is a living link with the rich knowledge of the landscape and of farming that Hardy himself valued so highly.

One of the things that I like about Ron's cows is that although they are quite a mixture of breeds apart from Dairy Shorthorns, they always seem to have horns, rather than being what Hardy called 'nott cows', or hornless, and this reminds me of a nice bit of rustic humour in *Tess of the D'Urbervilles*. Tess has just begun her new job as a milkmaid, and suddenly the cows seem to be milking less readily. The general opinion among the milkers is that this is due to the arrival of a new hand in their midst. ' "I've been told that it goes up into their horns at such times," said a dairy-maid.' Dairyman Crick was unsure: ' "I couldn't say, I certainly could not. But as nott cows will keep it back as well as the horned ones, I don't quite agree to it. Do you know that riddle about the nott cows, Jonathan? Why do nott cows give less milk in a year than horned?"

"I don't!" interposed the milkmaid. "Why do they?"

"Because there bain't so many of 'em,' said the dairyman.

Emminster

A view of Beaminster dominated by the church. This 'hill-surrounded little town', Hardy's Emminster, is full of associations.

It was where Angel Clare's parents lived and his father was the clergyman – 'a man of Apostolic simplicity in life and thought, he had in his raw youth made up his mind once for all on the deeper questions of existence, and admitted no further reasoning on them thenceforward'.

After months of hard labour on the farm at Flintcombe Ash, and having waited in vain for almost a year for some communication from her absent husband, Tess finally decided to apply to his parents for help, '. . . and there is no doubt that her dream at starting was to win the heart of her mother-in-law, tell her whole history to that lady, enlist her on her side and so gain back the truant.'

She left Flintcombe Ash at four on a Sunday morning and reached Emminster at about noon:

'The square tower, beneath which she knew that at that moment the Vicar and his congregation were gathered, had a severe look in her eyes. She wished that she had somehow contrived to come on a week-day. Such a good man might be prejudiced against a woman who had chosen Sunday, never realizing the necessities of her case. But it was incumbent upon her to go on now. She took off the thick boots in which she had walked thus far, put on her pretty thin ones of patent leather, and, stuffing the former into the hedge by the gate-post where she might readily find them again, descended the hill; the freshness of colour she had derived from the keen air thinning away in spite of her as she drew near the parsonage.'

Overhearing Angel's brothers talking about his 'ill-considered marriage', and though 'Her present condition was precisely one which would have enlisted the sympathies of old Mr and Mrs Clare', she abandons her plan to see them, deciding that 'there was nothing left for her to do but to continue upon that starve-acre farm till she could again summon courage to face the vicarage.'

Gertrude Bugler, who has contributed a preface to this book, and was Hardy's favourite 'Tess' in staged versions of the novel, lives just behind the church here, and the curator of Dorset County Museum, a treasure house of Hardy memorabilia, owns the house on the right of the sketch.

By extraordinary coincidence, it was in an antique shop here that, a few years ago, I found the beautiful cotton milkmaid's bonnet pictured here, just like those worn by Tess and others, as described in the harvest scene earlier.

The Wound

I climbed to the crest,
And, fog-festooned,
The sun lay west
Like a crimson wound:

Like that wound of mine
Of which none knew,
For I'd given no sign
That it pierced me through.

Here is a compact expression of the stoical attitude Hardy had determined to take in the face of what he saw as Emma Hardy's hurtful behaviour towards him. Some time before he had already written an eloquent testimony of the disappointment and sadness that exhausted love can bring:

There shall remain no trace
Of what so closely tied us,
And blank as ere love eyed us
Will be our meeting-place . . .

. . . Though fervent was our vow,
Though ruddily ran our pleasure,
Bliss has fulfilled its measure
And sees its sentence now.

Ache deep; but make no moans:
Smile out; but stilly suffer:
The paths of love are rougher
Than thoroughfares of stones.

After her death, filled with remorse at the neglect he had shown and, despite his second marriage, apparently endlessly mourning Emma (whom he now recognised as the love of his life), he was to recall,

That day when oats were reaped, and wheat was ripe, and barley ripening,
The road-dust hot, and the bleaching grasses dry,
I walked along and said,
While looking just ahead to where some silent people lie:

'I wounded one who's there, and now know well I wounded her;
But, ah, she does not know that she wounded me!'
And not an air stirred,
Nor a bill of any bird; and no response accorded she.

Dorchester – Casterbridge for Hardy – was the closest town of any size to where he lived, both as a boy and in his later days at Max Gate. Most of *The Mayor of Casterbridge* is set here, and the town also appears in six other novels as well as in numerous short stories and poems. Today, so much has changed that capturing anything of the atmosphere it must have had even a hundred years ago is well nigh impossible, so I have concentrated on some of the features that remain and that call up certain of the experiences of the characters in *The Mayor of Casterbridge*.

It is something of a surprise to discover that way back in 1910, when Hardy was presented with the freedom of Dorchester, he gave in his acceptance speech what turns out to have been a fairly accurate prediction of what the future held for the town:

'. . . my impression is that its tendency is to become more and more a residential spot, and that the nature of its business will be mainly that of administering to the wants of "private residents" as they are called . . . Dorchester's future will not be like its past; we may be sure of that. Like all other provincial towns, it will lose its individuality – has lost much of it already. We have become almost a London suburb owing to the quickened locomotion. . .'

Casterbridge, 'this antiquated borough', was 'untouched by the faintest sprinkle of modernism. It was compacted as a box of dominoes. It had no suburbs – in the ordinary sense. Country and town met at a mathematical line.'

One description in particular is tantalising in the extreme to any modern visitor to the town and leads one perhaps to believe him when he called Casterbridge 'not even the Dorchester as it existed sixty years ago, but a dream-place that never was outside an irresponsible book':

'When Elizabeth-Jane opened the hinged casement next morning the mellow air brought in the feel of imminent autumn almost as distinctly as if she had been in the remotest hamlet. Casterbridge was the complement of the rural life around; not its urban opposite. Bees and butterflies in the cornfields at the top of the town who desired to get to the meads at the bottom, took no circuitous course, but flew straight down High Street without any apparent consciousness that they were traversing strange latitudes. And in autumn airy spheres of thistledown floated into the same street, lodged upon the shop fronts, blew into drains, and innumerable tawny and yellow leaves skimmed along the pavement, and stole through people's doorways into their passages with a hesitating scratch on the floor, like the skirts of timid visitors.'

The reason given for this continuum between town and country is that the inhabitants of both are genuinely interdependent:

'Thus Casterbridge was in most respects but the pole, focus, or nerve-knot of the surrounding country life; differing from the many manufacturing towns which are as foreign bodies set down, like boulders on a plain, in a green world with which they have nothing in common. Casterbridge lived by agriculture at one remove further from the fountain-head than the adjoining villages – no more. The townsfolk understood every fluctuation in the rustic's condition, for it affected their receipts as much as the labourer's . . .'

As they first entered the town, Elizabeth Jane and her mother saw shop windows full of objects that revealed 'the agricultural and pastoral character of the people upon whom the town depended for its existence . . .' I have sketched a collection of the kinds of object they might well have seen. On the extreme right is a furze hook for cutting gorse to be used as poor man's fuel, then there are a couple of bill hooks, used in particular for hedge-laying but also for more general work; the reaping hook helped with a multitude of jobs – trimming round ditches, hedging and ditching work, small bits of hay-cutting. The tool that looks like a kind of double hoe is a root-chopper. In winter, once the root crops left for the sheep had been eaten down to the level of the ground, the remainder would be hooked out of the ground with a root-pecker (the two-pronged object) and then chopped up with the root-chopper. There are also a hay fork and two vessels made by the local Verwood Pottery: a Dorset owl, with the holes for a leather strap, and a 'field-flagon', both of which would have been used by farm-workers to take cider or other liquid refreshment into the fields with them.

The Antelope Hotel was where the coach that Lucetta took from Bristol to Budmouth changed horses. Having fallen in love with Michael Henchard and secured his promise that they would marry on condition that his first wife Susan did not reappear, Lucetta was thwarted by Susan's arrival in Casterbridge. After much reflection, she requested the return of any writings or 'trifling articles belonging to me' left in Henchard's possession, 'particularly the letters written in the first abandonment of feeling'. The rendez-vous at which he was to hand these over to her was The Antelope, but when the coach arrived, there was no sign of Lucetta, and Henchard returned home with the packet undelivered. When the letters were finally sent to her, and intercepted, they led, indirectly, to her death.

'What an old-fashioned place it seems to be!' said Elizabeth-Jane, when she and her mother looked down at Casterbridge as they approached the town for the first time. 'It is huddled all together; and it is shut in by a square hall of trees, like a plot of garden ground by a box edging.'

The 'square wall of trees' was the series of tree-lined avenues, planted on the ancient Roman walls of the town as promenades and known as 'the Walks'. When Henchard and his wife Susan first took up their relationship again, Susan lived in a cottage near one of the avenues to the west of the town, and many meetings between the characters took place on one or other of the Walks.

Shortly after Henchard's worst suspicions about the threat posed to him by his brilliant manager, Donald Farfrae, were confirmed, Farfrae decided to organise a 'day of public rejoicing' in celebration of 'a national event', and borrowed some 'rick cloths' from Henchard for the purpose. The Mayor, however, decided to put on the biggest and best entertainment the town had ever seen, but his lavish event was first rained off and then so badly attended that it was cancelled. Noticing that all the people out on the Walks that evening were promenading in the same direction, Henchard followed and found himself at 'a gigantic tent [that] had been ingeniously constructed without poles or ropes. The densest point of the sycamores had been selected, where the avenue of boughs made a closely interlaced vault overhead; to these boughs the canvas had been hung, and a barrel roof was the result . . . [Inside] a reel or fling of some sort was in progress; and the unusually sedate Farfrae was in the midst of the other dancers in the costume of a wild Highlander, flinging himself about and spinning to the tune. For a moment Henchard could not help laughing. Then he perceived the immense admiration for the Scotchman that revealed itself in the women's faces . . . All the town crowded to the Walk, such a delightful idea of a ballroom never having occurred to the inhabitants before.'

While waiting in the shadows to accompany his wife and daughter home, Henchard, already humiliated, overheard further unflattering comments about himself and resolved to rid himself of the man whom he had at one time regarded as his greatest asset.

Grey's Bridge was built by one of the family who lived in the old manor house at Kingston Maurward. In *The Mayor of Casterbridge*, it was described as being some way out of town, 'in fact, fairly in the meadows, though still within the town boundary'. It was different in character to the bridge closer in to town that was built of 'weather-stained brick', and was where 'those of lowest character' lingered when down on their luck: 'They had been of comparatively no account during their successes; and though they might feel dispirited, they had no particular sense of shame in their ruin.' By contrast, 'the *misérables* who would pause on the remoter bridge were of the politer stamp. They included bankrupts, hypochondriacs, persons who were what is called "out of situation" from fault or lucklessness, the inefficient of the professional class . . . The eyes of this species were mostly directed over the parapet upon the running water below . . . Some had been known to stand and think so long with this fixed gaze downward that eventually they had allowed their poor carcases to follow that gaze . . .'

This was the bridge, soon to become 'an accustomed halting place with him', to which Henchard came after being declared bankrupt, and where his erstwhile employee, Jopp, informed him that Lucetta and Farfrae had moved into his old home. On a later occasion, he set out from Grey's Bridge intending to commit suicide at Ten Hatches Weir.

Clearly Hardy, who would have used the bridge frequently, saw it as a setting of tragic possibility: it was also the place reached by the pregnant Fanny Robin one wet October evening as she struggled to complete her walk from Melchester to Casterbridge Union (the workhouse). Having virtually abandoned the attempt, exhausted, she crawled there, leaning on a large dog that appeared from nowhere to help her. Troy, who had earlier seen her on the road from a gig in which he was travelling with his wife Bathsheba, arranged to meet her at Grey's Bridge the following Monday morning, but in the interim she died in childbirth.

The Third Kissing Gate

This path leads across the meads from Stinsford Church to Dorchester, and I feel sure that it is the view you would have had while pausing at the little wooden gate immortalised by Hardy as 'The Third Kissing Gate':

> She foots it forward down the town,
> Then leaves the lamps behind,
> And trots along the eastern road
> Where elms stand double-lined.
>
> She clacks the first dim kissing-gate
> Beneath the storm-strained trees,
> And passes to the second mead
> That fringes Mellstock Leaze.
>
> She swings the second kissing-gate
> Next the gray garden-wall,
> And sees the third mead stretching down
> Towards the waterfall.
>
> And now the third-placed kissing-gate
> Her silent shadow nears,
> And touches with; when suddenly
> Her person disappears.
>
> What chanced by that third kissing-gate
> When the hushed mead grew dun?
> Lo – two dark figures clasped and closed
> As if they were but one.

'At the Wicket Gate', set in a similar position, describes a more dramatic meeting:

> There floated the sounds of church-chiming,
> But no one was nigh,
> Till there came, as a break in the loneness,
> Her father, she, I.
> And we slowly moved on to the wicket,
> And downlooking stood,
> Till anon people passed, and amid them
> We parted for good.
>
> Greater, wiser, may part there than we three
> Who parted there then,
> But never will Fates colder-featured
> Hold sway there again.
> Of the churchgoers through the still meadows
> No single one knew
> What a play was played under their eyes there
> As thence we withdrew.

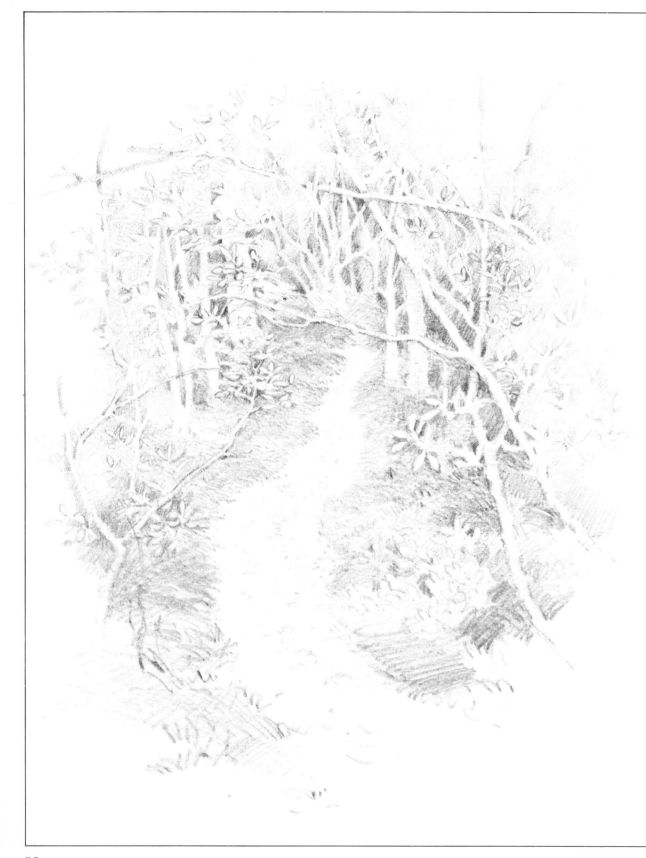

Snail-Creep

Having given up waiting for Fancy Day to come nutting with him on a rare half-day's holiday, Dick Dewy set off alone, and, after two miles' walk, reached 'a winding path called Snail-Creep [that] sloped up a hill and entered a hazel copse by a hole like a rabbit's burrow. In he plunged, vanished among the bushes, and in a short time there was no sign of his existence upon earth save an occasional rustling of boughs and snapping of twigs . . .' Dick gathered cob nuts at a furious pace, and by the time 'the sun had set, and bunches of nuts could not be distinguished from the leaves which vanished them', he had 'two pecks of the finest produce of the wood' in his bag.

Snail-Creep is a path that still exists in Grey's Wood, not far from Hardy's birthplace. This is a precious piece of mixed woodland, very similar to the larger Yellowham Wood, that can have changed little over the last two hundred years.

Hardy was as sensitive to the beauty and value of trees as he was to other parts of the countryside. 'Throwing a Tree', which sounds surprisingly modern, reveals him as an ardent conservationist:

The two executioners stalk along over the knolls,
Bearing two axes with heavy heads shining and wide,
And a long limp two-handled saw toothed for cutting great boles,
And so they approach the proud tree that bears the death-mark
    on its side.

Jackets doffed they swing axes and chop away just above ground,
And the chips fly about and lie white on the moss and fallen leaves;
Till a broad deep gash in the bark is hewn all the way round,
And one of them tries to hook upward a rope, which at last he achieves.

The saw then begins, till the top of the tall giant shivers:
The shivers are seen to grow greater each cut than before:
They edge out the saw, tug the rope; but the tree only quivers,
And kneeling and sawing again, they step back to try pulling once more.

Then, lastly, the living mast sways, further sways: with a shout
Job and Ike rush aside. Reached the end of its long staying powers
The tree crashes downward: it shakes all its neighbours throughout,
And two hundred years' steady growth has been ended in less
    than two hours.

Autumn

In *Interlopers at the Knap*, Hardy refers to countrymen being 'born . . . with only an open door between them and the four seasons', and the changing nature of the year is a constant theme in his writing. My imagination was caught by the poetry he wrote around autumnal images, and in particular by 'Last Week in October':

> The trees are undressing, and fling in many places –
> On the gray road, the roof, the window-sill –
> Their radiant robes and ribbons and yellow laces;
> A leaf each second so is flung at will,
> Here, there, another and another, still and still.
>
> A spider's web has caught one while downcoming,
> That stays there dangling when the rest pass on;
> Like a suspended criminal hangs he, murmuring
> In golden garb, while one yet green, high yon,
> Trembles, as fearing such a fate for himself anon.

'The Later Autumn' finds a melancholic aspect in the sights and sensations of this part of the year:

> Gone are the lovers, under the bush
> Stretched at their ease;
> Gone are the bees,
> Tangling themselves in your hair as they rush
> On the line of your track,
> Leg-laden, back
> With a dip to their hive
> In a prepossessed drive . . .
>
> Spinning leaves join the remains shrunk and brown
> Of last year's display
> That lie wasting away,
> On whose corpses they earlier as scorners gazed down
> From their aery green height:
> Now in the same plight
> They huddle; while yon
> A robin looks on.

This is a dramatic place on a stretch of coast which, when Hardy knew it, was empty and unspoilt. Small boats could be easily pulled up on to the shore, and the isolation and concealment of that area made it a perfect setting for smuggling. In *The Distracted Preacher*, Lizzy Newberry takes her admirer and would-be protector, the anxious and disapproving Mr Stockdale, to watch 'the run' at 'Lulwind Cove':

'The men remained quite silent when they reached the shore; and the next thing audible to the two at the top was the dip of heavy oars, and the dashing of waves against a boat's bow. In a moment the keel gently touched the shingle, and Stockdale heard the footsteps of the thirty-six carriers running forwards over the pebbles towards the point of landing.

'There was a sousing in the water as of a brood of ducks plunging in, showing that the men had not been particular about keeping their legs, or even their waists, dry from the brine: but it was impossible to see what they were doing, and in a few minutes the shingle was trampled again. The iron bar sustaining the rope, on which Stockdale's hand rested, began to swerve a little, and the carriers one by one appeared climbing up the sloping cliff, dripping audibly as they came, and sustaining themselves by the guide-rope. Each man on reaching the top was seen to be carrying a pair of tubs, one on his back and one on his chest, the two being slung together by cords passing round the chine hoops, and resting on the carrier's shoulders. Some of the strongest men carried three by putting an extra one on the top behind, but the customary load was a pair, these being quite weighty enough to give their bearer the sensation of having chest and backbone in contact after a walk of four or five miles.'

Having found most of the usual hiding places compromised, the smugglers are forced to 'sling the apple tree', a device for concealing smuggled goods that Hardy had heard of from an 'old carrier of "tubs" ' – an apple tree was planted in a tray or box which was then placed over the pit or cave.

Lulworth Cove is where Troy first walked and then swam, cast into 'a languor and depression greater than any he had experienced for many a day and year before' as a result of the death of Fanny Robin.

'Nothing moved in sky, land, or sea, except a frill of milkwhite foam along the nearer angles of the shores, shreds of which licked the contiguous stones like tongues. He descended and came to a small basin of sea enclosed by cliffs. Troy's nature freshened within him; he thought he would rest and bathe here before going further . . . Inside the cove the water was uninteresting to a swimmer, being smooth as a pond, and to get a little of the ocean swell Troy presently swam between the two projecting spurs of rock which formed the pillars of Hercules to this miniature Mediterranean. Unfortunately for Troy a current . . . existed outside and . . . [he] found himself carried to the left and then round in a swoop out to sea. He now recollected the place and its sinister character. Many bathers had there prayed for a dry death . . . [and] had been unanswered; and Troy began to deem it possible that he might be added to their number.'

He managed, however, to drift with the currents and was eventually rescued, though his wife, Bathsheba, presumed that he had drowned.

Many people in Dorset were involved in the illicit trade, and Hardy's grandfather, living in the cottage where Hardy was later born, was no exception: 'A whiplash across the window-pane would wake my grandfather at two or three in the morning, and he would dress and go down. . . Not a soul was there, but a heap of tubs loomed up in front of the door. He would set to work and stow them away in the dark closet aforesaid, and nothing more would happen till dusk the following evening, when groups of dark long-bearded fellows would arrive and carry off the tubs in two and fours slung over their shoulders.'

In *A Few Crusted Characters*, 'Lulwind Bay' is where the bodies of Stephen Hardcome and Olive, his cousin's wife, are cast ashore 'tightly locked in each other's arms, his lips upon hers, their features still wrapt in the calm and dream-like repose which had been observed in their demeanour as they glided along.'

In a poem entitled 'At Lulworth Cove a Century Back', Hardy commemorates a real visitor to the cove, Keats, who landed on the Dorset coast one day in September 1820 on his way to Rome and there composed the sonnet, 'Bright Star'. He also produced a fragment of instant legend about which he was later to feel somewhat uncomfortable. In 1804 a French invasion had been expected somewhere along the Dorset coast, and his short story *A Tradition of Eighteen Hundred and Four* recounts the sight of Napoleon, 'the Corsican ogre', landing at Lulworth Cove 'to examine these shores with a view to a practicable landing place': 'There was his bullet head, his short neck, his round yaller cheeks and chin, his gloomy face, and his great glaring eyes . . . and there was the forelock in the middle of his forehead, as in all the draughts of him.' Far from being recognised as a hoax, this picturesque account was hailed as a 'well-known tradition', leading Hardy to worry about 'whether a romancer was morally justified in going to extreme lengths of assurance . . . in respect of a tale he knew to be absolutely false' and he declared that were he still writing 'romances' he would now put at the beginning of each one: 'Understand that however true this book may be in essence, in fact it is utterly untrue'.

The Shepherd's Hut

This image comes from the early part of *Far from the Madding Crowd*. Having secured a lease twelve months before on a small downland sheep farm, 'enabled by sustained efforts of industry and chronic good spirits', Gabriel Oak is tending his ewes at lambing time and living in a shepherd's hut of the sort that was 'dragged into the fields when the lambing season comes on, to shelter the shepherd in his enforced nightly attendance.' Hardy describes one of Farmer Oak's excursions into the sheep fold to find a new-born lamb and then allows us to see inside the hut:

'The little speck of life he placed on a wisp of hay before the small stove, where a can of milk was simmering. Oak extinguished the lantern by blowing into it and then pinching the snuff, the cot being lighted by a candle suspended by a twisted wire. A rather hard couch, formed of a few corn sacks thrown carelessly down, covered half the floor of this little habitation, and here the young man stretched himself along, loosened his woollen cravat, and closed his eyes. In about the time a person unaccustomed to bodily labour would have decided upon which side to lie, Farmer Oak was asleep.

'The inside of the hut, as it now presented itself, was cosy and alluring, and the scarlet handful of fire in addition to the candle, reflecting its own genial colour upon whatever it could reach, flung associations of enjoyment even over utensils and tools. In the corner stood the sheep-crook, and along a shelf at one side were ranged bottles and canisters of the simple preparations pertaining to ovine surgery and physic; spirits of wine, turpentine, tar, magnesia, ginger, and castor-oil being the chief. On a triangular shelf across the corner stood bread, bacon, cheese, and a cup for ale or cider, which was supplied from a flagon beneath. Beside the provisions lay the flute, whose notes had lately been called forth by the lonely watcher to beguile a tedious hour. The house was ventilated by two round holes, like the lights of a ship's cabin, with wood slides.

'The lamb, revived by the warmth, began to bleat, and the sound entered Gabriel's ears and brain with an instant meaning, as expected sounds will. Passing from the profoundest sleep to the most alert wakefulness with the same ease that had accompanied the reverse operation, he looked at his watch, found that the hour-hand had shifted again, put on his hat, took the lamb in his arms, and carried it into the darkness. After placing the little creature with its mother he stood and carefully examined the sky, to ascertain the time of night from the altitude of the stars.'

This picture shows 'lonely Toller-Down', not far from Norcombe Hill. When I saw this landscape last summer, it fitted well with the description given by Hardy in *Far from the Madding Crowd* just before the sheep-shearing scene in the Great Barn:

'It was the first day in June, and the sheep-shearing season culminated, the landscape, even to the leanest pasture, being all health and colour. Every green was young, every pore was open and every stalk was swollen with racing currrents of juice. God was palpably present in the country, and the devil had gone with the world to town.'

Gabriel Oak's downland farm certainly took in Norcombe Hill and may well have encompassed Toller Down. This area, then, is where Oak was overtaken by the terrible catastrophe so heartrendingly described by Hardy:

'It was a still, moist night. Just before dawn he was assisted in waking by the abnormal reverberation of familiar music. To the shepherd, the note of the sheep-bell, like the ticking of the clock to other people, is a chronic sound that only makes itself noticed by ceasing or altering in some unusual manner from the well-known idle tinkle which signifies to the accustomed ear, however distant, that all is well in the fold. In the solemn calm of the awakening morn that note was heard by Gabriel, beating with unusual violence and rapidity. This exceptional ringing may be caused in two ways – by the rapid feeding of the sheep bearing the bell, as when the flock breaks into new pasture, which gives it an intermittent rapidity, or by the sheep starting off in a run, when the sound has a regular palpitation. The experienced ear of Oak knew the sound he now heard to be caused by the running of the flock with great velocity.

'He jumped out of bed, dressed, tore down the lane through a foggy dawn, and ascended the hill. The forward ewes were kept apart from those among which the fall of lambs would be later, there being two hundred of the latter class in Gabriel's flock. These two hundred seemed to have absolutely vanished from the hill. There were the fifty with their lambs, enclosed at the other end as he had left them, but the rest, forming the bulk of the flock, were nowhere. Gabriel called at the top of his voice the shepherd's call:
  "Ovey, ovey, ovey!"
'Not a single bleat. He went to the hedge: a gap had been broken through it, and in the gap were the footprints of the sheep. Rather surprised to find them break fence at this season, yet putting it down instantly to their great fondness for ivy in winter-time, of which a great deal grew in the plantation, he followed through the hedge. They were not in the plantation. He called again: the valleys and furthest hills resounded . . . but no sheep. He passed through the trees and along the ridge of the hill. On the extreme summit, where the ends of . . . two converging hedges . . . were stopped short by meeting the brow of the chalk-pit, he saw the younger dog standing against the sky – dark and motionless as Napoleon at St Helena.

'A horrible conviction darted through Oak. With a sensation of bodily faintness he advanced: at one point the rails were broken through, and there he saw the footprints of his ewes. The dog came up, licked his hand, and made signs implying that he expected some great reward for signal services rendered. Oak looked over the precipice. The ewes lay dead and dying at its foot – a heap of two hundred mangled carcases, representing in their condition just now at least two hundred more.'

After discovering this appalling disaster, Gabriel Oak's 'first feeling . . . was one of pity for the untimely fate of these gentle ewes and their unborn lambs.' But then he buckles at what it means to him: 'The sheep were not insured. All the savings of a frugal life had been dispersed at a blow; his hopes of being an independent farmer were laid low – possibly for ever . . . He leant down upon a rail and covered his face with his hands.'

Dorset horn sheep, or 'Old Wessex horns' as Hardy called them, made up the flock that Bathsheba Everdene asked Gabriel Oak to look after for her. Sheep were an essential part of farming in Dorset before the First World War, not just because of their wool and meat but also for fertilising land used for arable farming. Dorset horns were favoured because they were a strong breed which could walk daily from the water-meadows to the fields and seemed happy to be penned quite closely when they got there.

The lives of shepherds and the whole process of sheep-rearing always fascinated Hardy, and his enthusiasm led to an impressive knowledge of the subject. In the first draft of *Far from the Madding Crowd*, some of the meticulous technical description was cut (for fear that the text would be overloaded) including a detailed description of the effects of sheep rot that ran to several pages.

Good shepherds had traditionally commanded great respect in the countryside, but Hardy's admiration seems to have known no bounds. A small portrait study of a shepherd (now in the Dorset County Museum) hung on a wall close to his bed.

An Unkindly May

A shepherd stands by a gate in a white smock-frock:
He holds the gate ajar, intently counting his flock.

The sour spring wind is blurting boisterous-wise,
And bears on it dirty clouds across the skies;
Plantation timbers creak like rusty cranes,
And pigeons and rooks, dishevelled by late rains,
Are like gaunt vultures, sodden and unkempt,
And song-birds do not end what they attempt:
The buds have tried to open, but quite failing
Have pinched themselves together in their quailing.
The sun frowns whitely in eye-trying flaps
Through passing cloud-holes, mimicking audible taps.
'Nature, you're not commendable to-day!'
I think. 'Better to-morrow!' she seems to say.

That shepherd still stands in that white smock-frock,
Unnoting all things save the counting his flock.